D1474505

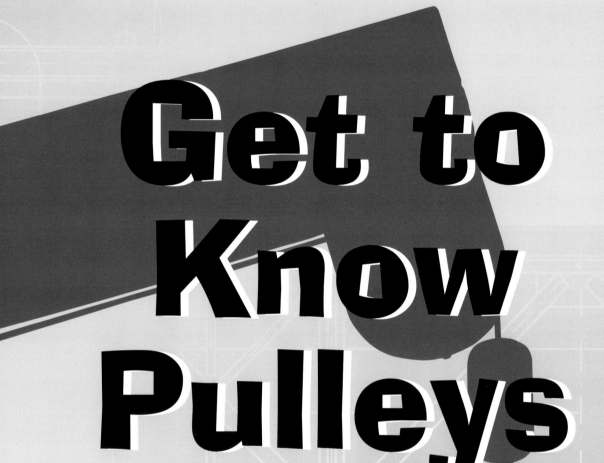

Get to Know Pulleys

by Karen Volpe

Crabtree Publishing Company
www.crabtreebooks.com

Crabtree Publishing Company

www.crabtreebooks.com

Author: Karen Volpe
Editors: Molly Aloian, Reagan Miller, Crystal Sikkens
Project coordinator: Robert Walker
Prepress technicians: Ken Wright, Margaret Amy Salter
Production coordinator: Margaret Amy Salter
Cover design: Samara Parent
Coordinating editor: Chester Fisher
Series and project editor: Penny Dowdy
Project manager: Kumar Kunal (Q2AMEDIA)
Art direction: Dibakar Acharjee (Q2AMEDIA)
Design: Ritu Chopra (Q2AMEDIA)
Photo research: Farheen Aadil (Q2AMEDIA)

Illustrations:
Robert MacGregor: page 24
Q2AMedia Art bank: pages 6, 7, 10, 11, 14, 15, 18, 19,
   22, 23, 26, 27

Photographs:
Alamy: Ken Hackett: p. 5
Corbis: Alan Schein Photography:
   p. 16 (bottom left); Christie's Images:
   p. 21
Gettyimages: Bob Thomas: p. 12
Ingram photo objects: p. 4 (lever)
Istockphoto: p. 8; Clayton Hansen:
   p. 4 (wheel and axle); Peeter Viisimaa:
   p. 9; Joris Van Caspel: p. 16 (top right);
   Loic Bernard: p. 28; Kriss Russell: p. 29
Shutterstock: Medvedev Andrey: p. 4 (screw);
   Andrjuss: p. 4 (wedge); Julián Rovagnati:
   p. 4 (inclined plane); Harley Molesworth:
   p. 4 (pulley), 31; Zack Frank: p. 13; Audrey
   Snider-Bell: p. 17; Andrew McDonough:
   p. 20; Michael Shake: p. 25

Library and Archives Canada Cataloguing in Publication

Volpe, Karen
   Get to know pulleys / Karen Volpe.

(Get to know simple machines)
Includes index.
ISBN 978-0-7787-4468-9 (bound).--ISBN 978-0-7787-4485-6 (pbk.)

   1. Pulleys--Juvenile literature.
I. Title. II. Series: Get to know simple machines

TJ1103.V64 2009   j621.8   C2009-900795-9

Library of Congress Cataloging-in-Publication Data

Volpe, Karen.
   Get to know pulleys / Karen Volpe.
      p. cm. -- (Get to know simple machines)
   Includes index.
   ISBN 978-0-7787-4485-6 (pbk. : alk. paper) -- ISBN 978-0-7787-4468-9
(reinforced library binding : alk. paper)
   1. Pulleys--Juvenile literature. I. Title. II. Series.

TJ1103.V65 2009
621.8--dc22

2009004585

Crabtree Publishing Company

www.crabtreebooks.com   1-800-387-7650

Published in Canada
Crabtree Publishing
616 Welland Ave.
St. Catharines, ON
L2M 5V6

Published in the United States
Crabtree Publishing
PMB16A
350 Fifth Ave., Suite 3308
New York, NY 10118

Published in the United Kingdom
Crabtree Publishing
White Cross Mills
High Town, Lancaster
LA1 4XS

Published in Australia
Crabtree Publishing
386 Mt. Alexander Rd.
Ascot Vale (Melbourne)
VIC 3032

Contents

What is a Simple Machine?

All people have jobs to do. Some jobs take a lot of **energy**. Energy is the ability to do **work**. Simple machines help people get jobs done without working too hard. This is called **mechanical advantage**.

Simple machines are tools that are made up of very few parts. There are six kinds of simple machines. They are inclined planes, levers, **pulleys**, wedges, screws, and wheels and axles.

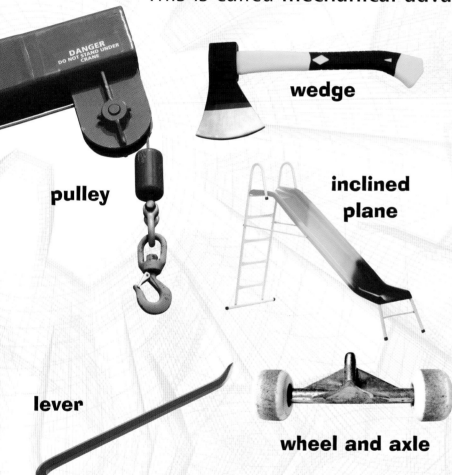

pulley

wedge

inclined plane

lever

wheel and axle

screw

These pictures show an example of each kind of simple machine.

One kind of simple machine is a pulley. A pulley is a wheel with a groove. A rope or chain fits into the groove. A pulley is used to lift or move objects.

You have probably seen pulleys on your blinds at home, on a clothesline, and even on a flagpole.

How a Pulley Makes Work Easier

You are trying to bring your lunch up to your tree house. Your hands are too full to climb the ladder. See how a pulley can help:

bucket

rope

snack

Tie a strong rope to the handle of a bucket. Fill the bucket with a **load** such as a snack.

Toss the other end of the rope over a tree branch close to your tree house. Ask a friend to wait in the tree house to receive the load.

Step 1

Step 2

Pull down on the rope to raise the bucket and load up. How does the rope and bucket pulley help you get your snack up to your tree house?

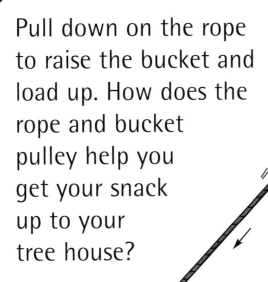

How has the rope and bucket pulley helped you do work? Did it make getting your snack up to your tree house easier? How do you raise the bucket? How do you lower it?

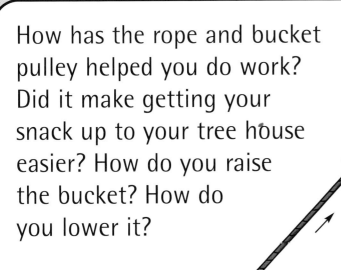

Fixed Pulleys

A **fixed pulley** does not move. It stays attached to a surface while the rope and load move. Fixed pulleys move a load in the opposite direction of the **force**. If you pull down on the rope, the load will go up.

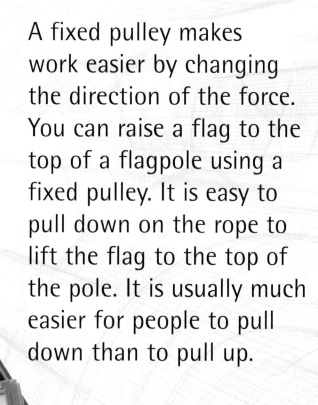

A fixed pulley makes work easier by changing the direction of the force. You can raise a flag to the top of a flagpole using a fixed pulley. It is easy to pull down on the rope to lift the flag to the top of the pole. It is usually much easier for people to pull down than to pull up.

This fixed pulley carries hay up to the hay loft.

When the boy pulls the rope, a bucket of water comes up.

People use fixed pulleys to gather fresh water from wells. A bucket hangs from the pulley to carry water up from deep under the ground.

9

Make a Fixed Pulley

You can make your own fixed pulley. You may need an adult to help. You will need:

wire coat hanger

spool

string

book

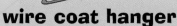

Get an adult to help you snip the bottom wire of the coat hanger. Put both wires through the spool. Bend the wires down so the spool turns easily and will not slide off.

Hang the coat hanger on a door knob or handle. Loop a long piece of string once around the spool.

Step 1

Step 2

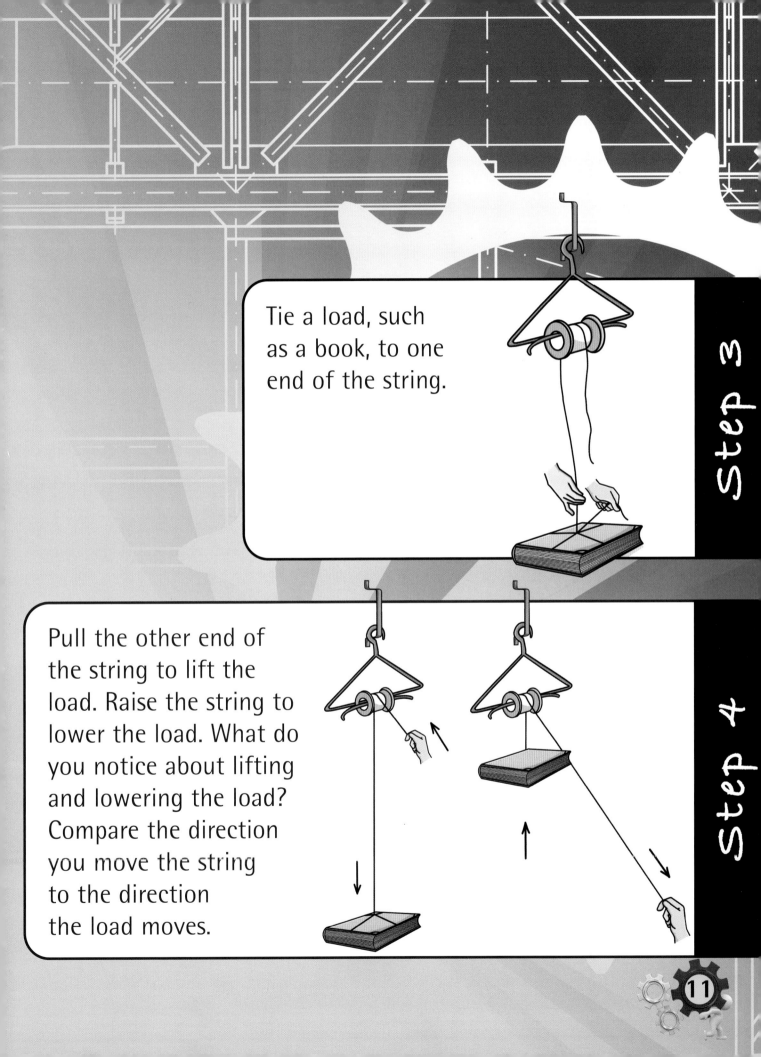

Tie a load, such as a book, to one end of the string.

Pull the other end of the string to lift the load. Raise the string to lower the load. What do you notice about lifting and lowering the load? Compare the direction you move the string to the direction the load moves.

11

Two or More Fixed Pulleys

Using two pulleys together decreases the **effort** needed to move a load. Adding more ropes and pulleys makes it even easier to lift the weight of a very heavy load.

Each rope holds a little bit of the load. This is like having a friend help you carry something heavy. The more help you have lifting the load, the lighter the load seems to be. Using two or more pulleys together helps you lift a bigger load.

With the help of a pulley, one man can raise a huge sail by himself.

12

Old Ironsides has over 250 lines of rope! Many are used to raise and lower sails.

The **USS Constitution**, also known as **Old Ironsides**, was built in 1797. Pulleys were used to lift the ship's sails when it was built, and they still do!

13

Broomstick Pulley

You can explore what happens when you use more pulleys. You will need:

two broom handles

two friends

ten feet (3-m) of heavy string

Tie one end of the string to one of the broom handles.

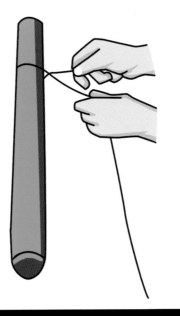

Have your two friends stand two and a half feet (0.8 m) apart holding the broom handles out in front of themselves.

Step 1

Step 2

Wrap the string around the broom handles twice.

Pull on the loose end of the string as your friends try to hold the broom handles apart. What happens to the broom handles? What happens to the string you pull? Try wrapping the string around the broom handles again and pull. What happens now?

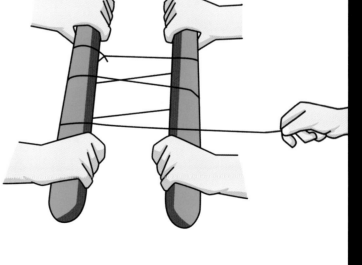

Moveable Pulleys

Moveable pulleys move along with the load. The load attaches under the pulley. Moveable pulleys decrease the effort needed to move a load. Both ends of the rope hold the load.

Window washers use pulleys to move up and down the sides of tall buildings.

One rope is tied to a fixed point. The other rope is pulled. Each rope holds half the weight of the load. When you pull the rope, you use half the effort to move the load. A moveable pulley helps move a large load using little effort.

A crane uses a strong cable instead of a rope or chain.

The rider wears a harness that attaches to the zip line pulley.

A zip line is a fun way to use a moveable pulley. You get to be the load! Strap on your safety gear and away you go!

Build a Moveable Pulley

Now we can build a moveable pulley. You will need:

a strong coat hanger

a small spool

string   **book**

Tie a string around the book and attach it firmly to the spool.

Tie a second piece of string to the bottom of the coat hanger. Loop the other end of the string around the spool.

Step 1

Step 2

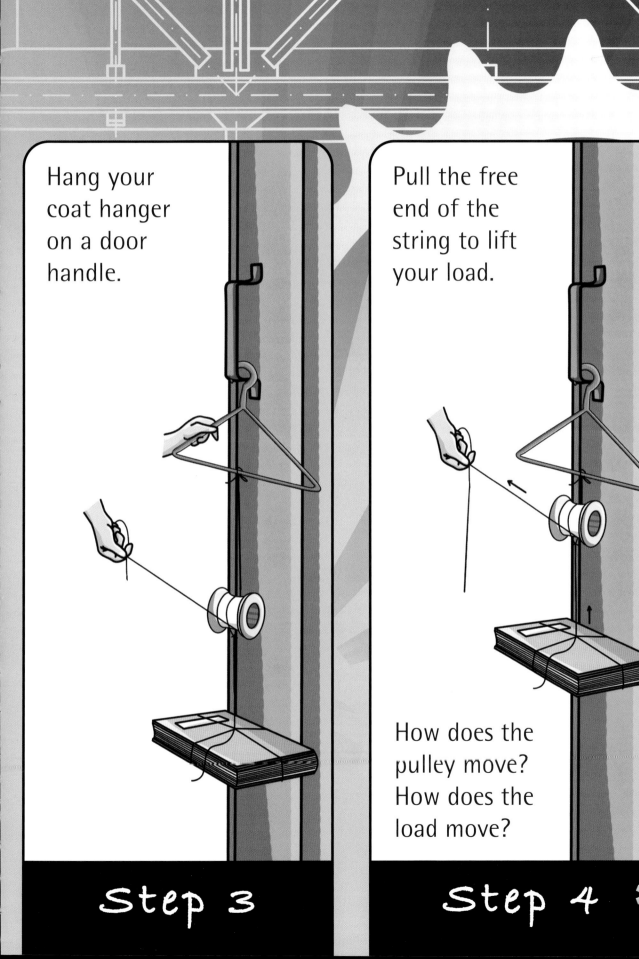

Hang your coat hanger on a door handle.

Pull the free end of the string to lift your load.

How does the pulley move? How does the load move?

Step 3

Step 4

19

Pulley Systems

Fixed and moveable pulleys can work together to move loads. A **pulley system** has two or more pulleys working as a team. A pulley system uses a small effort to move large loads.

Pulley systems can be very simple. Pulley systems can also be very **complex**. Adding more pulleys to a system makes it more complex. It also makes the work easier. One type of pulley system is the **block and tackle**. The block and tackle uses many fixed and moveable pulleys to lift very heavy loads. Big construction cranes use complex pulley systems to lift huge loads.

A crane uses fixed and moveable pulleys together to move heavy loads.

Tall cathedrals
were built
hundreds
of years ago.
There was no
construction
equipment to
help carry the
heavy loads.
Men and animals
pulled the ropes
of the pulley
system. This
lifted the heavy
columns and
beams used to
build cathedrals.

Workers lifted heavy
stones with pulleys to
build these columns.

Pulley Systems Make Work Easier

Let's explore how much more you can lift with some different pulley systems.

A pulley with one wheel allows you to lift 10 pounds (4.5 kg). A pulley with two wheels allows you to lift 20 pounds (9 kg). Each pulley added to the system lets you lift 10 more pounds. Continue the pattern.

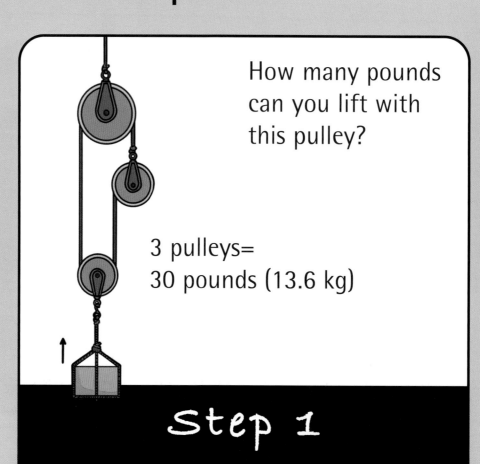

How many pounds can you lift with this pulley?

3 pulleys=
30 pounds (13.6 kg)

Step 1

How many pounds can
you lift with this pulley?

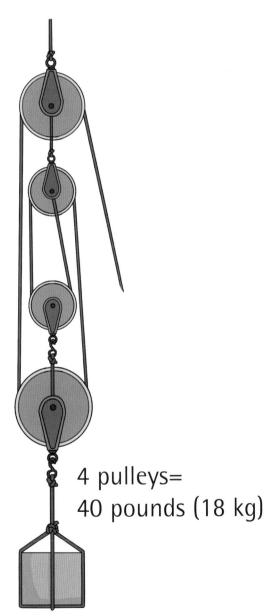

4 pulleys=
40 pounds (18 kg)

How many pounds can
you lift with this pulley?

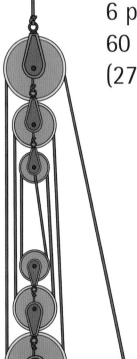

6 pulleys=
60 pounds
(27 kg)

Can you
predict how
many pounds
you could
lift with
eight pulleys?

Pulleys All Around You

You can find pulleys all around you. They might look different than the wheel and rope pulley used in this book. Pulleys can have **belts** or chains that help do work. Any wheel turned by a belt, rope, or chain is a pulley.

Some pulleys are inside machines where we may not be able to see them. Motors often use belts. For example, the motor inside a washing machine uses a belt to move the washing machine basket.

A bicycle chain makes the wheels on your bicycle move.

Can you find the pulleys in this engine?

FACT BOX

Pulleys are even used to help a car engine run! Pulleys help move many parts inside a car engine, such as the fans that keep the car engine from getting too hot.

Pulleys in Real Life

Explore your home to find pulleys. Some pulleys may look a little different. Others may be hidden. How many pulleys can you find ...

...in your living room?

Do you have window blinds that can be raised and lowered? What about drapes that are pulled open and closed? Do you see a grandfather clock with weights inside?

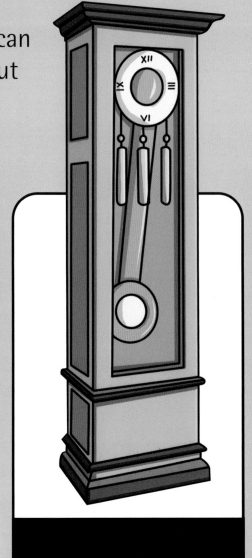

...outside?

Do you see a clothesline? Can you find a flagpole at your home or school?

...in your garage?

Can you find a pulley on your bicycle? Can you find a pulley on an automatic garage door?

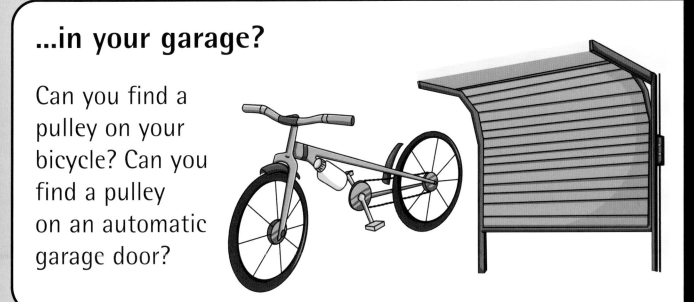

Simple Machines Working Together

Simple machines can work together to do work. A machine made up of two or more simple machines is called a **complex machine**. Many complex machines include pulleys.

A car is a complex machine. Many parts move together to do work. The pulley is part of a motor. One pulley helps blow air in the air conditioner. Another helps move the wheels.

Pulleys work with other simple machines to move this ski lift.

An elevator is a complex machine. Levers are used to open and close the doors. Elevators also use pulley systems to move people up or down several floors in seconds.

Find simple and complex machines around you. What work do thcy do?

29

Glossary

belt A band of strong flexible material

block and tackle A pulley system that combines fixed and moveable pulleys

cathedral A place of worship

complex Made up of many parts

complex machine Two or more simple machines working together

effort The push or pull you use to move an object

energy The ability to do work

fixed pulley A pulley that does not move; it changes the direction of a force

force A push or pull

harness A system of straps that is worn by a person to support his or her weight

load The object to be moved

mechanical advantage How much easier and faster a machine makes work

moveable pulley A pulley that moves with the load; it decreases the amount of effort needed to move a load

pulley A wheel with a groove and rope, belt, or chain

pulley system Two or more pulleys working as a team

work When a push or pull moves an object

pulley

Index

Web Sites

www.edheads.org/activities/simple-machines/

www.mos.org/sln/Leonardo/InventorsToolbox.html

www.mikids.com/Smachines.htm

teacher.scholastic.com/dirtrep/simple/index.htm

Printed in the U.S.A. — CG